# Donna Brandes and Howard Phillips

# Gamesters' Handbook

## 140 Games for Teachers and Group Leaders

HUTCHINSON

London Melbourne Sydney Auckland Johannesburg

Hutchinson & Co. (Publishers) Ltd
An imprint of the Hutchinson Publishing Group
24 Highbury Crescent, London N5 1RX

Hutchinson Group (Australia) Pty Ltd
30–32 Cremorne Street, Richmond South, Victoria 3121
PO Box 151, Broadway, New South Wales 2007

Hutchinson Group (NZ) Ltd
32–34 View Road, PO Box 40–086, Glenfield, Auckland 10

Hutchinson Group (SA) (Pty) Ltd
PO Box 337, Bergvlei 2012, South Africa

First published by The Growth Centre (Tyneside)
54 St George's Terrace, Newcastle Upon Tyne, 1977

Published by Hutchinson in ring-binder 1978

Paperback first published by Hutchinson 1979
Reprinted 1979 and 1980 (twice)

© Donna Brandes and Howard Phillips 1977

Designed by Walter Truman-Cox FSIA

Printed in Great Britain by The Anchor Press Ltd
and bound by Wm Brendon & Son Ltd
both of Tiptree, Essex

ISBN 0 09 136421 3

Also available in ring-binder (ISBN 0 09 136420 5)

# Contents

# Introduction

## Games Games Games

The games in this book offer a valuable source of activities, exercises and strategies for parents, group leaders, people planning parties, travellers, in fact for anyone who might wish to enliven any occasion they choose. Anyone can use the games since they can be used with different levels of skill. They can be used either simply, just for fun and enjoyment, or with greater point promoting specific aims.

The ability of many of our games to help people relax socially on both a one-to-one basis and with a group, encourages the use of the games by teachers and group leaders. This use is further enhanced by aims noted on each activity and outlining the value of the game in different developmental directions.

# Games in school

Games offer flexibility: flexibility of approach, of programme, of aims It is through this flexibility that a serious attempt can be made to develop an all round programme of personal growth. Particular aims can be fulfilled through the use of specific games in controlled directions. These can be integrated in a general plan which can then give the teacher an overall view of what is happening and what is being developed within their subject.

Games can be used constructively and not as a series of stop gap lessons or as pointless activities. Each game can have a different purpose which can always be defined — even 'fun' is purposeful.

Games can sort out problems, the kind of problems found in inter-personal relationships. They can help social inadequacy by developing co-operation within groups; develop sensitivity to the problems of others through games needing trust, and promote inter-dependency as well as an independence of personal identity.

Games can help break down artificial barriers between subjects. Simulation and improvisations provide an opportunity to extend links between subject or interest areas, and games can act as a catalyst for this. Role playing through games can extend their use in any number of directions in all subjects. Adapting games to suit a particular use is easy, especially for those familiar with 'Drama' teaching: care must be taken, however, to vary the games 'menu' and not continually dish up the same old meal with a different garnish. The size of the games selection should be useful here.

Games generate interest: they need enthusiasm. Used with purpose and effect they can be the framework upon which all other work is developed.

# Games for groups

Games offer the promotion of effective communication. The usefulness of games in this direction cannot be over-emphasised. By helping people to relax in groups, games can promote the flow of communication between complete strangers and particularly shy people who need added encouragement. Additionally, hostilities can be broken down and undesirable barriers removed.

During the development of group work, games can be used in an impromptu way to extend or clarify a particular area of response. By introducing a game, the group leader can add positive reinforcement to previous ideas or add divergent ideas through analogy.

Many group discussions can be hindered by lack of 'focus'. A well chosen game can add focus to a topic or development area. This also has the added effect of stimulating the development in a refreshing way.

The added attraction in the 'role playing' aspects of many games give group members more security in which to develop their ideas and express themselves. Therefore, games can provide readily adaptable structures in which the ideas of the participants can experience growth gradually within the experience of the game and the shelter of its format.

Finally the enjoyment which can be generated by games does more than anything to develop a group identity. This fun can act as the basic ingredient for any group work and can develop cohesion and an open, accepting atmosphere much more readily than any other way.

Groups need games.

# The Handbook

In compiling the games we have tried to include selections from different areas of our work so that the user can benefit from our collective classroom experience (25 years teaching) and Donna's extensive training and experience in group dynamics and Gestalt therapy. The games themselves can be used easily without any previous specialised knowledge. Each one has been found to work successfully in a number of different situations.

To further aid the developmental aspect of the games we have included a section outlining our basic teaching strategies used in conjunction with the games. The purpose of the basic strategies is to develop greater independence of action together with a realisation of the responsibility that this brings personally and socially.

We have sectioned the game into four main types:
Social, Personal, Concentrative and Introductory.

The sections, however, are to be used only as a guide. Many of the games have a number of uses, some of which transcend specified sections. The games, therefore, are sectionalised for the benefit of the user through bias only and not through any strict division of material. Social and Personal Development sections are self explanatory in their material. The Introductory section is used primarily for warm up exercises, but also for concluding activities too. Because of this they are often quite short. Concentrative games are used when people need to focus their attention on either a mental or a physical problem requiring skilful development.

The Handbook itself is used simply. Games can be chosen from each alphabetical section and can be used either in conjunction with one another, or independently. The games can be detached from the handbook and used separately. If this is to be done regularly we recommend that you reinforce favourite games with gummed rings or strips of transparent adhesive tape. Teachers might also like to use the games number on their record sheets so that a greater diversification of materials can be used.

# Acknowledgement of sources

We have been using these games in our work with many kinds of groups. They have grown with us over the years, and their sources have been wide and various. Their growth has also involved adaptation, evolution, integration, extension, variation, so that it is no longer possible to identify sources for most of the games. Games can not be copyrighted, so that our own games, as well as games which we have obtained from other books, are open for use by anyone. Many times we have "invented" a game for an occasion, only to find it later in a book, and vice versa.

Among the books which have been most useful to us are those of Sidney Simon, William Schutz, John Stevens.

We are especially indebted to Steve Myers, of Mt. View, California, for his pioneering work in Human Development in schools.

# Basic strategies

## The waiting game

This approach removes a great deal of the need for discipline and attention getting devices on the part of the teacher. Tell the group that you are not going to fight for their attention or quiet, that whenever they are together as a group for instruction or discussion, you will just wait until they are ready to listen. Tell them that it is called 'The Waiting Game', and that you will not take the responsibility for their attention, that they must take it themselves. (Note: I have seen this used with very small children, five year olds. After the first few lessons, they will get themselves and each other quiet, with no reminders from the leader).

The leader's waiting must have a quality of nothingness..... no resignation or martyred patience: all questions and interruptions must be ignored. It must be a non-threatening attitude as well; do not worry about the time you are wasting. If you persevere with them in the beginning, you will save great quantities of time and effort later.

Remember, the idea behind the Waiting Game is that the group takes all responsibility for how they are behaving, not the leader. If they use Drama time at first to chat with each other, they will soon get bored and express a preference for active happenings. So think of something else while you are waiting, plan your dinner menus or tomorrow's lesson or recite 'How do I love thee? Let me count the ways'.

You must be patient and consistent and play it every time, or it will not work.

# 'The circle' or 'rounds'

Sitting in a circle, rather than in rows of chairs or in a random setting, can influence group dynamics. It gives everyone the same status, including the leader, and it exposes each one's face to everyone else, and allows eye contact: therefore, a great many activities in this compendium are played or experienced in a circle.

The circle must be understood and experienced as a safe place, a place where one can speak freely about his opinions or feelings without the risk of being laughed at or judged.

Therefore, when groups are sitting in the circle, the leader must make sure that the freedom of the situation is understood to be contained in a safe structure.

A 'round' is a time when each person in the circle, progressing around the circle in turn, makes a statement completing one of the following sentences (or others of your own devising):
I noticed .......... (particularly good for films, etc.)
I discovered .......... (especially after a new experience or game)
I wish ..........
I learned ..........

Resent and Appreciate .......... this is highly recommended for evaluation of an experience. One round of 'I resent ..........', followed by a round of 'I appreciate' .........., for negative and positive feelings, in that order.

When doing rounds, everyone who is not actually the speaker, must listen quietly, and no comments are to be made, even by the leader. If a statement is made which does necessitate discussion, this should be saved until after the rounds are completed. Anyone can refuse a turn by saying: 'I pass', and there should be no comment about this either.

This structure can be used for many purposes, including the following:
Evaluation
To discuss an experience, a film, a play, a game just played
Planning, class meetings, problem solving
Positive reinforcement

# Brainstorming

The object of brainstorming is to generate a great many useful ideas on any subject or problem in a short period of time; it is also very useful for producing possible material for writing or discussion.

Suppose a class is looking for potential places to take a field trip. The leader places a blackboard at the front of the group, and asks for ideas. He writes down every idea, without comment, discarding nothing. If ideas are slow to come, he can put some of his own down, but he should wait before doing so. Once the ideas begin coming, they tend to come very quickly.

When ideas have stopped flowing, he stops writing, and pointing to each asks how many people think that that one has possibilities, erasing the ones that have no votes at all, unless someone wants to discuss them. Now the remaining possibilities are discussed in detail, and finally one is chosen by voting.

Remember:
No negative evaluation of any idea is to be made by the leader.
Work for quantity, not quality: the longer the list, the better.
Encourage zany, far-out ideas.

A secondary objective for brainstorming is to unite the group. This happens, usually, if the brainstorming session is properly led, because each person has had a chance to contribute, and is made to feel that his idea is at least worth writing down. It turns group problem-solving away from a competitive atmosphere where people are contending to have their own ideas accepted, and towards a collaborative venture where the problem itself is the prime adversary, and not another member of the group.

If a group has not experienced brainstorming before, it is a good idea to introduce it with the following games:

Continued overleaf

### Coke bottle

Leader has blackboard and chalk, or large chart paper and felt pen.

Leader says: 'Imagine that you are on a desert island. There is plenty of food and shelter, but only one man-made object, a COCA-COLA bottle. Using your wildest imaginations, think of as many uses as you possibly can for that coke bottle'. The leader then writes down the ideas as fast as group members can call them out, omitting none, and writing them completely at random so that no ranking is possible. No one should comment on any ideas until all of them are written. The leader can also put in ideas, thus remaining a contributing member of the group.

### 1001 uses of a shoe

Same as above, but an element of competition is introduced by brainstorming in teams (using a shoe instead of a coke bottle, as this game is often used as a follow-up to 'Coke Bottle'). Each team is given a leader, paper and pencil, and three minutes to brainstorm, then their ideas are counted. Another two minutes, and count the total. One last minute period, and the total for each team is announced. The teams then are allowed a few minutes to come to a group decision about which are their five most original ideas, i.e. the ones that the other team will not have. The teams sit together and read the five they have chosen. Points are given for any ideas which have not been thought of by any other team.

# Ask them policy

Whatever problems or concerns you are having with any given group, they are not your problems, they are the group's problems: do not try to solve them at home in bed at night, or in the staff room. Tell the problem to the group and ask for ideas or feelings about it. Remember, you are as much a member of the group as anyone else; you should share your feelings and problems with them if you want real group interaction.

# Social development

## Contents

S1 **Air-raid shelter**

**Materials**    None

**Aims**    Role-playing, group decision-making, group interaction.

**Procedure**    Divide in groups of 8 — 10. Each group member adopts a specific role, usually an occupation, e.g. a doctor, an athlete, a teacher, movie-star, mother, housewife, etc. (These can be written out and picked from a hat). Tell groups they are in an air-raid shelter after an atom bomb has fallen, big enough and with enough air and food for only six people, therefore they must get rid of several members. Each group member must argue as to why he should be allowed to survive. A group decision must be reached as to who goes and stays: no suicides or murder allowed. Set a time limit for the decision. Later discuss how the group interacted making the decision, whether each person played an active or passive role, how satisfied each was with his role, etc.

**Variations**    Instead of an air-raid shelter, have a life raft or desert island or space ship. Add incidents, accidents, rituals, funerals, ceremonies.

S2

# Backward fall & catch

**Materials**    None

**Aims**    Trust development, relaxation

**Procedure**    Partners stand a relative distance, one person behind the other, but both facing the same direction. The person in front allows himself the fall back and be caught by his rear partner. The front person must be relaxed. Distance can be varied within a safe limit.

**Variations**    One person stands between two and falls backwards and forwards. The person is propelled to an upright position each time. To be successful the subject must be relaxed.

Group of about six or seven stand in close circle. Subject stands in the centre and allows himself to fall backwards and forwards, sideways, etc. Participants may gently propel subject into the upright position, or towards another member of the circle. It is important that the subject stays in the centre and that he is relaxed with eyes closed and feet stationary.

S3

# Body lift

**Materials**   None

**Aims**   Trust, concentration, group development

**Procedure**   Group chooses each member in turn and elevates them to a horizontal position above the heads of the group. The person is held there for a specific period, and then lowered carefully to the floor. The elevated person must relax and close eyes.

It is often a good idea to have the groups raise and lower in unison. This often avoids confusion and helps concentration.

**Variations**   Vary speed and control of lift, — walk, rock, etc. Have the person involved give instructions to the group. Combine with S2 Backward fall & catch.

S4

# Clay Island

**Materials**   Enough clay for each group of seven people to gather around a round or square table and work together. Clay should be malleable, non-drying variety; also leaves, twigs and tooth-picks, or sticks should be provided.

**Aims**   Group interaction, role playing, creativity.

**Procedure**   a   Groups of 5 — 7 gather around a table or on the floor with a large lump of clay in the centre. Spend 10 minutes pounding, pushing, slapping clay into large, soft, formless mass. Encourage energetic pounding of the clay. Together, form the lump into an island, adding terrain, coves, caves, mountains, rivers. (Non-verbal).

b   Without talking, stake out a territory on the island for yourself, mark boundaries, build a shelter or home, and improve as desired.

c   Hold an island council meeting, elect leader, make whatever decisions group deems necessary for survival or interaction on the island. (Give these directions one step at a time).

Can stop here and go into discussion of the group interaction, or go further (see variations).

**Variations**   Continue with small groups, improvising incidents of island life. Can be done with large paper and chalk instead of clay.

S5

# Conveyor belt

**Materials**     None

**Aims**     Trust, group development

**Procedure**     Two lines of people facing each other (about two feet apart). Try to have people of similar height opposite. First couple detach and one person lies on back between first six/eight people. The person is lifted to head height and is then slowly passed down the whole length of the chain. The person is carefully lowered to the ground at the end. Better results if the person relaxes and closes eyes.

S6          # D.U.E. Depth unfolding experience

**Materials**      None

**Aims**        Trust building, self-disclosure, getting to know each other

**Procedure**    Groups of no more than eight. Each person has six minutes
to talk about himself. Emphasise those things you
particularly would like new people to know about you. (No
feedback is given at this time.) Afterwards, use a group
interview, or a feedback session giving first impressions, or a
strength bombardment.

S7     # Fear in a hat

**Materials**     Pencil, paper, 'hat' (or tin, etc.)

**Aims**     Share and accept

**Procedure**     Played in a circle. Ask everyone, including leader, to complete this sentence: (anonymously) 'In this class (or group, or whatever) I am afraid that ..........' Put the scraps of paper in the tin or receptacle in the centre. Pass the tin around, stopping at each person while he draws one out and reads it, enlarging on the sentence and trying to express what the person was feeling. (For example, the leader reads the first one, and might say 'In this class I am afraid that I will be laughed at ..........(continues talking) I am afraid to say my feelings because everyone laughs at me, so I never say anything.') Continue around the circle. Leader must make sure that everyone just listens, and does not comment. No arguing or comment is allowed. Then discuss what was noticed or discovered.

**Variations**     Likes and dislikes in a hat (two tins)

Worries in a hat

Gripes in a hat

Wishes in a hat, etc.

S8

# Group interview

**Materials**    None

**Aims**    Trust building, self-disclosure, self-awareness, reflective listening.

**Procedure**    Sit in a circle, one volunteer is the focus of the group. Anyone may ask any questions of the focal person. He may answer honestly, or say 'I'd rather not answer that.' The purpose of the questions should be to get to know the person on a more than superficial level. Questioners tend to become more skilful with experience. Leader must work to prevent the group from arguing or criticizing the focal person — it is just time to listen and accept. Leader can direct the questions to a deeper level than just biographical facts by asking questions which require thought, philosophy, opinions, feelings, etc. A possible closing question is: 'Is there something else you'd like us to know about you?' Continue as long as group maintains interest. Interview other members throughout the course.

**Variations**    Do rounds of questions. Do short interviews of several people. Let everyone be the focus at one, ask each other questions.

S9                    **Guess who said it**

**Materials**         None

**Aims**              Give and accept positive feedback, trust building

**Procedure**         Played in a circle. One person leaves the room. Three or
                      four people make positive statements about him,
                      trying to include specialised information that not everyone
                      might know about the person. When he returns, he stands
                      in a circle, and the statements are repeated to him one at a
                      time, while he tries to guess who said each one. (Leader
                      insists on receiving only positive statements).

S10      # Head rest & roll

**Materials**      None

**Aims**      Trust, concentration, relaxation

**Procedure**      One partner lies on the floor and relaxes. Other partner supports his head and slowly manipulates it from left to right. Prone partner must allow his neck muscles to relax and be fully supported. (very difficult) Care must be taken that trust is broad-based in this activity. Successes in this difficult activity must be noted.

S11     **It's obvious**

**Materials**     None

**Aims**     Trust building, awareness of how we look at other people, ice-breaker.

**Procedure**     Break into groups of 4 or 5, sit in a small circle with your group. Focus on one person, have each person in the group look at A and start a sentence with 'It's obvious that you......' Make sure it is something obvious, like an item of clothing — no inferences allowed here. Do the same for B, C, D etc. Start again, take a closer look, start a sentence with 'I see that you.......' This would be something that you might not notice at first glance, but only on looking more closely. Go all the way around. Start again with 'I imagine that you.......' Here you are allowed guesses, inferences, wild imaginings. Check the imaginings with the focal person: 'Is that right?' Discuss the experience in the small groups. Join the large group for a round of 'I discovered .......'

**Variations**     Do more imaginings about other people in your group. Write the imaginings.

S12 # Mental gifts

**Materials**  Pencil, two or three small pieces of paper each

**Aims**  Trust building, positive feedback, learning to give and take compliments or suggestions.

**Procedure**  a  (If large blackboards are available.)
Write each group member's name at the top of a section of the board. Everyone walks around writing mental gifts in each person's section. They should be something you think the person would like, or something you think they should have. Example: 'I give you the gift of appreciating your own wisdom'.

b  (If no blackboards)
Everyone writes his name on four or five scraps of paper. These are put into a hat or dish: each member draws five out and addresses gifts to those names. At a signal everyone delivers their gifts. They can be shared aloud, if desired.

**Variations**  1  On festive occasions, i.e. pre-cut Valentine hearts, paper Christmas trees, Easter eggs, etc., to write the gifts on.

2  Repeat this at intervals during the course. Try to see that gifts become more relevant to the needs of the receiver.

S13        # Parties

**Materials**      None

**Aims**          Characterisation, improvisation

**Procedure**     Have improvisation of rich people's parties, poor people parties, student's parties, re-unions (i.e. jail breakers re-unions, any re-unions, etc.) It is a good idea to have the group decide what kind of a party it wants. Each person (or with a partner) decides who they are and what they have to say at this party. Discuss who, (they are going as) what they are looking forward to doing there, etc. Have a person announce each newcomer, or pair of people as they arrive. It is worth while discussing the whole thing afterwards with regard to:

    **a** whether objective was achieved

    **b** what was real/unreal about it

    **c** why we interpret these kind of people in this kind of way

**Variations**    Develop to show racial, national, political, relationships etc.

S14 **Partner conversations**

**Materials**    None

**Aims**    Trust building, imagination, fun

**Procedure**    Get a partner, hold hands or put arms around each other. Find another pair, and hold a conversation with them, each partner alternating in speaking one word, until a sentence is formed. (It becomes an exercise in mind-reading.)

**Variations**    Use teams (3 or 4) instead of pairs.

S15

# Pass the buck

**Materials**      The Buck (a pen, glove, pack of cigarettes, etc.)

**Aims**          Control group interaction, concentration

**Procedure**     Leader holds the Buck, says no one can speak unless they are holding it. Pass it to the next person in the circle, or to whoever raises his hand to speak.

**Variations**    Toss it quickly back and forth: *must* speak when you have it or you are out. Use it to tell stories: whoever has the Buck must continue.

**Social development**
Communication
Movement, body skills
Warm-up, ice-breaker
Trust, sensitivity

S16      **Pile-up**

**Materials**      None

**Aims**      Warm up, group development, trust

**Procedure**      Members of the group lie on their stomachs and close their eyes. All start crawling towards central point and they meet. They crawl over each other until pile starts to form in the centre. When pile is complete, all open eyes.

**Variations**      Blindfold 'bumps': Group is blindfolded and walks to the centre to form a knot.

S17      # Resent & appreciate

**Materials**     None

**Aims**     Evaluation, problem solving, expression of feeling, trust building.

**Procedure**   

a   In a circle. Each person makes a statement beginning with 'I resent ......' (ordinarily, in relation to the work just completed, or the experience in the class or group.)

b   Repeat the round, beginning with 'I appreciate......'

c   Before starting, make sure that everyone understands the meaning of both words. *No one is allowed to comment.*

d   Anyone can say 'I pass', which means 'No comment.'

e   Anyone can say: 'I resent nothing', or 'I appreciate nothing.'

**Note**     This is not an ordinary game, but a most crucial one. It is used for evaluation purposes throughout any course or group work.

S18

# The rule of the game

**Materials**    None

**Aims**    Group interaction, imagination, intellectual exercise, fun, getting to know each other.

**Procedure**    Circle: one person goes out, others choose a rule. When he comes back he must find out the rule by asking people questions about themselves. A good rule to begin with: answer every question as if you were the person on your right. Players must answer questions honestly, according to the rules. Another example: all girls tell lies, all men tell the truth.

Rules can be hard or very simple, according to age and experience. Rules can be visual (scratch head before answering), or structural (each answer begins with the next letter of the alphabet).

S19      # Sabotage

**Materials**      None

**Aims**      Awareness of group dynamics, breaking down barriers, trust building, empathy. Good opening exercise.

**Procedure**    **a** Discuss meaning of sabotage as opposed to destruction (sabotage is subtle, covert).

     **b** Do a round of: 'I could sabotage this group by.......' or, do a round of things we say that sabotage ourselves, e.g. 'I'm too tired, 'I've done this before'.

     **c** Divide in threes. A tells B one of his own problems. B just listens, nods, encourages. B does *not* try to solve problem). C tries to sabotage the communication, interrupts, etc., trying to be as subtle as possible. Change roles until each has experienced each role. Do a round of: 'I discovered.......'

     **d** Do a round of: 'I could help this group by.......', or, things we say that help us to be part of the group, e.g. 'Today I'll really listen.'

**Variations**      Use non-verbal sabotage, or invent other forms.

## S20  Sitting circle

| | |
|---|---|
| **Materials** | Circle of over 25 people |
| **Aims** | Trust, fun |

**Procedure**

a Group stands in a close circle, in queue form, with right shoulders towards the centre of the circle.

b Circle closes so that everyone is touching the person in front and behind them.

c Participants hold the waist of the person in front

d Everyone bends their knees until they feel themselves supported on the knee of the person behind.

e If successful (rare first time) the whole group is self-supported, each person sitting on the knee of the person behind.

**Note**

This can only be successful if the circular shape is maintained throughout and it is helpful if the group leans *slightly* towards the centre as they are trying to settle down.

**Variations**

*After secure sitting position is achieved*

1 Everyone leans inwards slightly and raises left leg

2 All stretch arms in unison

3 Try alternate stepping with right and left feet, (very difficult.)

S21      **Structures**

**Materials**      None

**Aims**      Trust, concentration, body control

**Procedure**      Leader split group into small units. Each unit (2 − 8) constructs a particular structure by linking themselves together.

Ideas      Make a suspension bridge
an arched bridge
a tree
a crane
a modern building
an aeroplane/helicopter
a car/truck/bus
a ship
an antenna
a tower
a dome
a temple
a cathedral

**Variations**      Move around without falling

S22          # Territories

**Materials**   None

**Aims**        Values clarification, self-validation, group and social
                development.

**Procedure**   Discuss how the world is broken up into different countries
                or states, and how each state makes its own laws within its
                boundaries. Each group or individual marks off a territory,
                using chairs, tables, etc., and makes its own laws.  After
                discussion this can lead to various improvisations within each
                territory.  Leader can suggest that improvisation is based
                upon someone who breaks one of the laws, or on a stranger
                who visits the new territory, etc.

**Variations**  One group could become the authority in a particular state
                and the rest of the group has to do as they are told.

                Ideas must be worked out beforehand however, or else the
                leader must take an active role as one of the citizens.

                Territories can be fantasy places, outer space, etc.

S23

# Teacher-student fantasy

**Materials**  Small groups or pairs

**Aims**  Social development, improvisation, role-playing, values development

**Procedure**  a  Each pair sits facing each other, and closes their eyes.

b  Each person thinks back over his school career, and remembers the 'worst teacher he ever had'. Remember in detail, all the annoying or destructive behaviours of that teacher.

c  Partners open their eyes and take turns talking to that worst teacher, using the partner as the 'target', and telling him off, saying all the things they would never dare say in person.

d  Discuss that experience.

e  Follow the same procedure with the 'best teacher'.

f  In the large group, do a round of 'I discovered' or 'I noticed'.

**Variations**  1  Make the conversations into improvisations.

2  Brainstorm qualities of 'bad' and 'good' teachers.

3  Choose one of the negative qualities and follow-up on it, applying it to yourself, doing a value continuum (P58 Value Continuum).

S24 **True story**

**Materials**    None

**Aims**    Self-disclosure, trust building, listening skills

**Procedure**  a  'A' tells a partner of a true incident that happened to him

b  Partner 'B' repeats it, trying to keep the same inflection and emphasis that A had.

c  A takes on a different role, (e.g. an absent-minded old woman) and tells or enacts the story again.

d  A and B discuss the experience

e  Switch and repeat

**Variations**    A and B enact each others' stories

S25      # Trust walk

**Materials**      Blindfolds (optional), outdoor area preferred

**Aims**      Trust building, sensory awareness

**Procedure**      Emphasise that this is a *non-verbal* experience. Choose a partner that you would like to know better. A closes eyes (or is blindfolded), B leads him and helps him to experience the world around through his other four senses. Communicate with each other through touch. Protect your partner, let him know you care, be very gentle, try to give him a truly *beautiful* experience. After 15 — 30 minutes, switch roles. After an equal time, lead your partner back here. Discuss the experience with your partner, then join the group and do a round of 'I discovered.......'

**Variations**      There are many other 'blind' experiences described elsewhere in this collection.

S26            # Two & two make one

**Materials**      None

**Aims**           Trust, personal development

**Procedure**      Leader asks the group to space out.  Each person to see how
                   far he can lean over without falling.  People then pair up and
                   see what a difference another's support can make in
                   repeating the exercise.

                   Discuss observations afterwards.  Draw comparisons

S27

# Verbal boxing

**Materials**  Stop watch or clock

**Aims**  Overcome shyness, warm-up for drama, fun, imagination

**Procedure**  One challenger faces another in the centre for a 30 second bout: the group decides who has won, a third person can challenge the winner.

'Bouts' fall into categories:

a  Insults: colourful and inventive *untrue* insults should be encouraged; no 'hitting below the belt' with truth or weakness: this is in the form of a conversation.

b  Long-windedness: the challenger must keep up a *continuous* stream of talk, both at the same time.

c  Gibberish: give challengers an emotion to express, (e.g. fear), must be expressed with nonsense sounds: both talking at once.

**Variations**  Invent new categories

S28      # Wall crash

**Materials**      None

**Aims**      Trust, group development, self-validation, personal development.

**Procedure**

a   Whole group forms a queue

b   Leader chooses two people to act as safety nets, they stand near the wall opposite the queue.

c   The person at the front of the queue walks, eyes closed, towards the wall.

d   'Safety nets' catch him before he hits the wall

e   After each person has had a turn at a walking pace, the pace is speeded up on each turn, until the person is running at full speed.

The point is that the trust develops through a feeling of safety each time the person is caught by the 'safety nets', so that, in the end, he feels safe even when he is running.

S29

# What do they want?

**Materials**     None

**Aims**     Values development, social awareness, trust

**Procedure**     Start with a round and discuss the way in which people group together: i.e. family, friends, school, college, housing estate, town region, nation. *Also:* Religion, Politics, Race.

Round splits into groups of about eight. Each group forms itself under one of the above categories divided in the initial round.

Leader acts as devil's advocate and/or mediator between groups. Verbal conflict is to be desired and control must be exercised to maintain this: emotions are expected to run high. Groups must re-assemble afterwards into a round and plenty of time must be left for discussion.

Note     This strategy can be a major contribution to the development of the above themes.

**Variations**     Smaller units can be used: i.e. partners.

S30    **Whose face**

**Materials**    Blindfolds for the whole group

**Aims**    Concentration, inter-personal development

**Procedure**    Partners sit facing each other and examine each other's facial features, both visually and with finger tips. Gentleness must be emphasised.

Afterwards one partner is blindfolded and they have to discover their partner from the main group. The other partner is then blindfolded and the activity is repeated.

**Variations**    Both partners are blindfolded and they have to find each other.

S31     # Who's missing?

**Materials**     Small prizes, such as sweets. (optional)

**Aims**     Memory training, concentration, building groups, fun.

**Procedure**     Group is seated, scattered around the room, one person, A goes out. The group moves around, changing places, and one more person, B, leaves by the other door, or hides. A returns and has 30 seconds to guess who's missing. If he does he wins (a small sweet, if you wish to give prizes), if he doesn't B wins.

**Variations**     Add consequences for the loser

S32      # The word wizard

**Materials**     Pencil and paper

**Aims**     Imagination, communication, group interaction, fun

**Procedure**     (The instructions below are given slowly, and one at a time, with pauses between.)

Leader says: 'I am a wizard, I am taking away all your words. But as I am generous, you may have four of them back. Write down the four words you want to keep out of all the words in the world. Find a partner, communicate using *only* your four words, plus gestures....... (pause). Now you may share words with your partner, write down his words. Now you have up to eight words. Change partners and communicate with these words on your list only. Share words. Repeat, changing partners 4 to 6 times. Now take your list and try to write a poem using just those words.'

# Personal development

## Contents

P33   # Advertisements

**Materials**     Pencil and paper each

**Aims**          Self-disclosure, positive feedback, group trust building.
                  (Group should know each other a while before playing this).

**Procedure**     Write an advertisement describing and selling yourself as a
                  friend. (Twenty five words or less). Keep in mind: why
                  would someone want to buy (choose) you rather than
                  another friend? Put ads. in a hat, pass around, read aloud
                  one at a time, guess who wrote each (be able to say *why* you
                  guessed that person). Do a round of 'I noticed..........'

**Variations**    1 Advertisements of self as a parent, teacher, pupil, son/
                  daughter, brother/sister, lover, sweetheart, etc.

                  2 Put large ads. on the wall, write ads. for other people.

                  3 Illustrate or make cartoons of the ads.

P34     **Auctions**

**Materials**     None

**Aims**     Develop self-confidence, imagination

**Procedure**     Each member of the group decides to auction an imaginary object and after some time at individual preparation, (optional) group members improvise a sale of the object. Each member of the group should take part as an auctioneer.

**Variations**     Class brings in articles for mock or even real auction.

P35          **Blind dinner**

**Materials**     Group members bring unusual foods, cut in small pieces,
                  arranged on paper plates. Be sure there are also things to
                  drink.

**Aims**          Sensory awareness, trust building, fun.

**Procedure**  a  Sit at tables, close eyes, pass things around and sample them.
                  *Non-verbal.*

               b  Spread things on large table, walk around and feed each
                  other samples. *Non-verbal.*

               c  Help yourself to a plateful, sit down alone, close eyes, taste
                  and savour samples in silence.

               d  Sit in circle, close eyes, have a few people passing things to
                  taste. (See that they also get a tasting turn.)

**Variations**    Do several times, different ways, use foreign foods, cheese
                  and wine, fruits and nuts, etc.

P36      # American charades

**Materials**      Paper, pencils, watch with second hand

**Aims**      Fun, communication, non-verbal communication, drama

**Procedure**    a   Divide into two teams and go into separate rooms

b   Write on slips of paper, song titles, film titles, books, famous people, famous sayings, plays, etc.

c   Come back into same room, sit with your team, send one person for a slip of paper from the other team.

d   Act out the title on the paper for your own team, according to the structure outlined below, while someone keeps time. After 3 minutes, time is up, and someone from the other team gets a piece of paper and tries.

e   The team with lowest time elapsed at the end, wins. So a cumulative score of minutes and seconds for each team is kept.

Structure      for acting out titles. (You cannot talk)

1   Show your team what the title is with agreed sign e.g.
movie: crank the camera
play: pull the curtains,
**Everyone on your team shouts out the answers.**

2   Show with fingers, number of words

3   Show with fingers, which word you are starting with

4   Fingers on wrist indicate number of syllables and also which syllable, if necessary.

5   Begin acting out words

6   Other signals can be made up and agreed upon, such as 'Little words', 'Big words', 'Whole idea', 'Shorten word', 'Lengthen word', 'Rhymes with', etc.

| P37 | # Coat of arms |

**Materials**      Paper, pencils, scissors, felt pens, or chalk.

**Aims**           Self-awareness, self-disclosure

**Procedure**      Show examples of heraldry and coats of arms, discuss symbolism. Design your own coat of arms; suggestions below are only optional, it is best if people invent their own. (The suggestions are also just ideas; people invent their own symbols.) Afterwards, share and discuss.

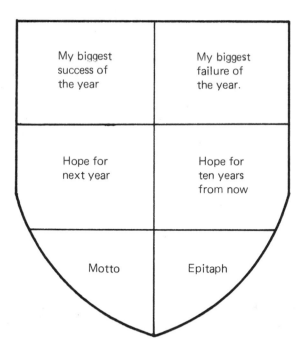

**Variations**      Make huge ones for the whole group

P38            # Continuing story

**Materials**     None

**Aims**        Confidence, communication, imagination

**Procedure**     One group of about four people decide on the theme of a
story. They begin to develop this story and the characters
they have chosen. At a given point the leader substitutes four
other people to take over the rules of the original four and
continue the story. There may be slight variations in this as
one character may leave the story and a different one may
enter. One point must be stressed however, and that is
continuing of:

a   character
b   theme

and also a continuation of the story until the group finishes
the last story off. This is a useful activity to discuss
constructively afterwards.

Example theme   Crazy races
The Haunted House
The Escape
The Funfair
Crazy Sports

Length of individual contribution can be varied and story
thus speeded or slowed.

**Variations**    Story can expand with extra people so that no-one drops out
and eventually the whole group is included. Discuss centre of
action and how it moved with new entrants.

P39        **Control tower**

**Materials**     Blindfolds, chairs, books, other obstacles

**Aims**          Trust building, awareness, fun

**Procedure**  a  Blindfold **A** (plane): **B** (the control tower) guides him verbally through an obstacle course (runway) which has been set up between two rows of chairs.

b  **A** gets one penalty point each time he touches an obstacle.

c  When he has five points, he 'crashes', and **B** crashes with him. They are out.

d  Another pair starts; the obstacles are changed around.

**Variations**    Use human obstacles. Play in teams

P40

# Don't make me laugh

| | |
|---|---|
| **Materials** | None |
| **Aims** | Personal development, fun, concentration |
| **Procedure** | One partner becomes a serious character and decides he will never laugh or even smile again. The other partner has to change this state of affairs. The leader will have to decide whether tickling, etc., is allowed. Partners exchange roles when the first partner does laugh. |
| **Variations** | Make partner angry instead. No hurting though, no blows or personal comments. Discuss afterwards. |

P41      # Feeling cards

**Materials**      Blackboard, felt pen, strips and cardboard about 3" x 7" (brightly coloured if possible).

**Aims**      Become aware of feelings, learn feeling vocabulary, become accustomed to showing and discussing feelings.

**Procedure**    a   Brainstorm (see 'Brainstorming' page 11) feeling words. Leader writes these words on coloured cards.

         b   Leader holds up a card, (e.g. card says 'embarrassed' or 'hateful'). Members complete sentence using word: 'I feel embarrassed when ………'

         c   Groups of three, pick words at random, make mime or short play using all the three words (feelings).

         d   Relate true experiences: 'The last time I felt really embarrassed was when ……….'

         e   Speak for someone else, check accuracy. Example: (Sally is speaking for Joan): 'I'm Joan and I feel embarrassed when I'm asked to speak out in class. Is that true Joan?' Joan answers and discusses Sally's statement.

**Variations**    1   Have people choose (or make) cards which describe their feelings right now. Discuss.

         2   Use cards to inspire essays, poetry, art; hang cards on wall. Have members make up games using the cards.

P42      # Fists

**Materials**      None

**Aims**      Sound relationships, self-validation

**Procedure**      One person in each pair closes his fists tightly and the other person tries to persuade him to open them. After a reasonable time the partners exchange roles.

Instruction      'Only open your fist if you feel you have really been persuaded by your partner'.

**Variations**      1 Partner One coils body, and the other person has to straighten it out.

2 Partner holds his own feet

3 Partner clenches his teeth

Note      No form of violence is allowed, although threats may be used.

P43                   # Gripes auction

**Materials**         A card or piece of paper for each person and pencils

**Aims**              Self-validation, social development, values clarification

**Procedure**        The leader holds a series of cards, each containing a gripe.
                     (see below). All the gripes are read out first and then each
                     gripe is put up for auction. Each person has 100 points to
                     spend and cannot bid over this. When the auction is over the
                     people who have cards explain why their particular gripe is
                     important and how it affects their lives.

                     A sheet of paper should be reserved to note the number of
                     points each gripe is sold for. This is to check on the points
                     each person spends.

| **List of gripes** | Dogs | Vandalism |
|---|---|---|
| Little children | The Weather | Drama Lessons |
| Baby sitting | Pocket Money | School Dances |
| Smokers | School Meals | Dentists |
| Films on T.V. | Sports | Violence |
| Newspapers | Cats | Television |
| Parents | Homework | Town Council |
| School | Books | Policemen |
| Brothers | Teachers | Fashions |
| Sisters | Grandparents | Shopping |
| Youth Club | Pollution | Doctors |
| Holidays | | |
| Gossips | | |
| Facilities for young people (recreation) | | |

**Variations**       Brainstorm list of gripes first

P44     # Group yell

**Materials**     None

**Aims**     Release tension, warm-up, trust building

**Procedure**     Group huddle together in crouching position. Leader begins a low hum. As the group begins to rise slowly, the sound level also rises, so that at the end, everyone leaps into the air and shouts at the same time.

Repeat until everyone has really *shouted* at the end.

**Variations**     Add specific words or sounds chosen by the group in advance.

P45          # Hell

**Materials**    None (although suitable music and rostrum blocks are helpful).

**Aims**         Improvisation, fun, group leadership, personal development

**Procedure**    Whole group discusses various torments and evil which abound in hell. Also the sounds and the visual impact of such a scene. Pairs and threes act various torments. Eventually (with possible music stimulus) whole group joins and the torments change partners and move among the tormented. This situation is reversed later so that everyone has been given a place on each side.

Try to improvise torments particularly suited to members of the group.

**Variations**   1  One person can be the devil for a day and order and direct the group.

2  Try to develop more sophisticated tensions or torments. (Relate to everyday tensions which can build up.)

3  Discuss various ideas about Heaven, and repeat the above processes.

*Suitable music which can be used: Ride of the Valkyrie, Rite of Spring.*

P46      # I am a shoe

**Materials**      None

**Aims**      Mixing, self-disclosure, self-awareness

**Procedure**      Sit silently, look around the room and choose any object. Think what it would be like to be that. Name three qualities it possesses. (e.g. I am a shoe, I am warm, soft and comfortable). Go around the room introducing yourself that way and shaking hands. Now sit down, think briefly about whether those qualities describe you. Give the object your own name, and walk around introducing yourself that way. I am Susan, I am warm, soft, and comfortable.) Make a circle and discuss the experience, doing a round of 'I felt ..........', or 'I discovered..........'

**Variations**      Write a story as if you were the object, or tell one aloud. Find a partner and discuss the qualities you chose, in relation to yourself and your partner.

P47          # Lawyer

**Materials**      None, chairs in a circle

**Aims**          Concentration, sharpening of wits, fun

**Procedure**     The Lawyer stands in the centre, says to the players,
'Starting now, you must not answer when I speak to you,
the person on your left must answer for you. You must not
nod, or smile, or respond to me in any way. Do you
understand?' The players almost invariably answer, and they
would be out .......... The Lawyer starts again, asking each
person questions and putting them out if they answer. To
progress to the next rule and make it more sophisticated, no
one may answer 'Yes' or 'No' .......... New rules may be added
as you go along.

P48          # Memory game

**Materials**     A tray, with twelve assorted objects, a scarf or towel, pencil
                  and paper.

**Aims**          Memory training, observation, concentration

**Procedure**     Leader previously has assembled twelve objects on a tray
                  (e.g. hairbrush, stapler, clock, etc.) and covered the tray with
                  a towel. Gather the group around, unveil the tray, and give
                  them 30 seconds to silently observe the tray. Cover the tray
                  and have them list as many objects as they can remember.

**Variations**    Give small prizes (a sweet) for the most listed. Remove one
                  object from the tray, give a prize for the first person who can
                  tell what is missing.

P49

# Merry-go-round

**Materials**      None

**Aims**      Lead up to improvisation, role-playing, fun

**Procedure**  **a** Two people begin improvising a scene, on any subject. (e.g. a burglar and a policeman).
They are Number 1 and Number 2.

**b** After the scene is well established, any one from the audience may come up and start a new scene; he is Number 3 and must change the subject completely. (Perhaps he might be a surgeon and begin talking about the operation taking place.)

**c** Number 1 has to find a reason to leave, in the context of the scene, leaving Numbers 2 and 3 together.

**d** Number 4 comes up, changing the subject again. Number 2 finds a reason to leave.

**e** The game continues as long as it is fresh and lively.

P50            # News & goods

**Materials**      None

**Aims**           Warm-up, self-validation, self-disclosure, trust building

**Procedure**      As a round: start a sentence with 'The nicest thing that
                   happened to me this week was ..........' Emphasize that it
                   might be something big and exciting or small and pleasant.
                   (Perhaps just a smile from someone special.)

**Variations**     Write them anonymously, guess who wrote them. Sometimes
                   do 'Bad News': 'The worst thing that happened to me this
                   week was ..........' (Follow this with 'Good News'.). Some-
                   times do Bad News and discuss the degree of sympathy
                   desired.

**Personal development**
Group relations
Trust, sensitivity
Communication,
Self-disclosure
Confidence building

P51

# Parent cocktail party

**Materials**    None

**Aims**    Identify parental attitudes, develop role-playing techniques

**Procedure**    Become one of your parents. Pretend you are at a party.
Move around the room, talking to the people you meet about
your child (or children). Be sure you talk to many different
people and listen to them as well. Return to the circle: do a
round of 'I discovered ..........'

**Variations**    1  Sit in a circle and make the parental statements as a round

2  Be your other parent. Be you, discussing your parents

3  Be a favourite teacher, then a much-disliked teacher

4  Values continuum on relationships with parents

P52          # Projections ahead

**Materials**      None

**Aims**         Self-validation

**Procedure**     Each person envisages themselves at a particular point in the
                future. They think how life will be for them and using other
                members of their group, take turns in relating how they see
                themselves. Leader chooses their point in time, i.e., five
                years, ten years, etc. and also orientation, i.e.

          **a** with family
          **b** at work, etc.

                The leader must state clearly whether this activity is to be as
                the person sees himself really, or as he wishes himself to be.
                If the leader thinks group comment is valuable, then care
                must be taken to ensure that the comments are positive
                and not demeaning.

**Variations**    1 Groups could develop one or more of their ideas into an
                improvisation.

                2 Projections can be written down, discussed: could be
                national or world projections — including the person.

**Personal development**
Social development
Confidence building
Trust sensitivity
Communication,
Self-disclosure

P53

# Road map

**Materials**     Large sheet of paper per person and pencil or felt tip

**Aims**     Self-validation

**Procedure**     Each person is asked to make a road map of their life so far. Beginning with birth and extending to the present. Each map should somehow show the good places (either scenic or open road, etc.) or the bad places (bumpy spots, etc.), hospital (road works etc.)  Also barriers, detours, and the general direction of their present course.

Compare life's past course with your imagined future, i.e., goals, etc.  How will they be achieved? What has made the good spots?

**Variations**     1  Extend and project the map into the future. (conjecture or daydream)

2  Construct lists of positive and negative problems and events. Decide on points systems, i.e., + and −, and evaluate your life.

3  Role-play passing detours, etc.

P54          # Speakeasy

**Materials**      One chair

**Aims**          Self-validation, group development

**Procedure**      A chair is placed in front of the group. Each person has a chance to sit on the chair and talk to the group. They can develop any subject of their choice. It is often better to start out with descriptions of themselves — group leader setting the pace by going first.

This is a very important activity which can become a permanent feature of each drama lesson, especially if a drama lesson is over 60 minutes long.

Positive developments can result in group discussion and ways of resolving problems.

**Variations**      Speak on controversial subjects, give views, then discuss, argue, do values continuum, etc.

P55      **This is your life**

**Materials**     None

**Aims**     Self-disclosure, trust building, role-playing, lead up to improvisation.

**Procedure**     One person volunteers to be the director, and selects a story from his own life, which he tells to the group. The group then re-enacts the scene, under the director's supervision. Discuss, then choose a new director.

**Variations**     If the group knows each other well, people can tell and direct scenes from other people's lives.

P56 **Turning points**

**Materials** None

**Aims** Self-validation

**Procedure** Each person is asked to remember a particular point in their past. They remember what happened at that particular point and using other members of their groups, take turns relating this experience. The leader chooses the particular point, i.e. something that happened ........., 5 years ago and the orientation, i.e. :

a with family
b with friends
c at school, etc.

The leader may ask for the most important point in their lives. If the leader thinks that group comment is valuable, then care must be taken to ensure that the comments are sympathetic, constructive and understanding.

**Variations** Groups could develop one or more of these into an improvisation. This can be constructed as in 'Statues', or in which ever way the group wants to do it. A time limit is advisable. Ideas can be written down and evaluated in groups.

**Personal development**
Communication,
Self-disclolsure
Trust, sensitivity
Social development
Confidence building

P57          # Uniqueness cards

**Materials**      One card or piece of paper for each person, pencils

**Aims**           Self-validation, communication, other-awareness

**Procedure**      Each person is given a card or piece of paper and asked to
write a description of themselves. The description must be
written in such a way that it could be no other person in
the group. It is better to describe ideas and personality
rather than physical appearance. Each person reads their
description out to the group. There will probably be many
descriptions which are not particularly unique. Have the
members of the group revise their descriptions and find out
how they really are unique. Goal is that no-one could say
'That's just like me!'

**Variations**     Write a card for someone else.

P58          # Value continuum

**Materials**       None

**Aims**           Self-validation, values clarification, communication,
                   reflective listening.

**Procedure**      Leader and group decide on the subject to be evaluated.
                   Subjects might be:

                   tidiness — untidiness
                   school's great — school's lousy
                   eat anything — very choosy
                   miser — spendthrift
                   T.V. always — T.V. never
                   wants no friends — wants everyone to be their friend
                   decision maker — decision avoider
                   100% happy — 100% unhappy
                   never argue — always argue
                   always follows others — individualist

**Note**           **topics can be much more sophisticated than the ones shown
                   above**

                   One corner of the room is designated for the people of one
                   extreme point of view and the next corner for the people of
                   the opposite extreme view. Each person is then invited to
                   place themselves, according to their opinion or practice,
                   somewhere along the imaginary scale of degrees, on or
                   between the two extremes. If two or more people wish to
                   share the same point they can queue or sit outwards from the
                   wall.

                   This 'declaration' can be used for discussion. As in other
                   games no criticism is to be made of the person's choice.

**Variations**   1 Each person chooses where he would like to be, not
                   necessarily where he would be in reality.

                 2 Each person explains why they are choosing a particular
                   point.

                 3 Split continuum into two and have a dialogue between the
                   two sides on 'why we are right!'

P59

# Walk my walk

**Materials**        None

**Aims**        Self awareness, observation, lead up to movement

**Procedure**        Stand in a large circle, leaving plenty of space in the middle.
A volunteer walks across the circle several times, others
observe his walk and comment on it. (Be sure comments are
supportive and analytical: e.g. 'His shoulders are straight,
his arms don't swing, etc.) Now everyone tries his walk,
trying to really get into the feeling of being that person.
Give as many volunteers a turn as possible, while interest
holds.

**Variations**        Take on roles and walk in them: spy, aged person, jellyfish,
etc.

# Concentrative development

## Contents

C60        **Addabout**

**Materials**      None

**Aims**      Concentration, memory, mine techniques

**Procedure**      Sit in a circle.  Leader stands, makes one simple movement,
e.g.; spiral movement with finger.  Next person makes
spiral movement plus another, e.g. foot stamp, etc., adding
while continuing around the circle. No talking, if someone
misses or talks, he's out.

**Variations**      Have the group invent a new rule

## C61    Add your emotions

**Materials**      None

**Aims**        Inter-personal development, improvisation

**Procedure**    Each group decides on a theme for a short improvisation. They then choose (or are given) three emotions to include in the story, so that the story progresses from the first emotion, through to the second, and finishes on the third.

e.g. worry .......... panic .......... relief (theme: fire)

When the groups work through the improvisation, and develop their ideas physically, they then develop three tableaux, each representing the emotion concerned. When the tableaux are shown to the whole group they should show the story seen in three 'frozen' pictures each demonstrating the particular emotion apparent at the point of the story. The story must also be apparent so that the tableaux also represent: *beginning, climax, conclusion.*

Some themes     a fire
watching a football game
a fight
attacked by a lion
ski-ing for the first time
*themes basically invented by groups*

Some emotions

| | | |
|---|---|---|
| pain | amusement | terror |
| pleasure | displeasure | fright |
| contempt | astonishment | loathing |
| weariness | indifference | degradation |
| triumph | impatience | alarm |
| horror | grief | worry |
| fear | excitement | shame |
| hatred | relief | |

**Variations**    Choose themes from group suggestions. Let them decide emotions.

**Concentrative development**
Movement, body skills
Drama training
Communication
Social development
Trust, sensitivity

C62

# Adverb game

**Materials**    None

**Aims**    Spontaneous reactions, imagination, fun, improvisation

**Procedure**    One person leaves the room, others choose an adverb, e.g. 'slowly'. When he returns he must find out what the adverb is by asking people to do things 'that way', e.g. 'Shake hands that way', (so they would shake hands very slowly.) If you don't want to, or can't do what he says, you say 'I don't want to', (very slowly). After each command he makes a guess at the word: he can continue until he guesses or gives up.

**Variations**    Leader calls out adverbs, e.g. 'nervously', and everyone moves around the room that way. (This is good as a follow-up activity, and to move into an active game or drama.)

C63      # Blind explore

**Materials**      None (blindfolds could be used)

**Aims**      Sensory awareness, trust building, warming-up in new group

**Procedure**      Darken the room if possible and also close eyes. Move slowly, gently around the room. (No talking: emphasize it is non-verbal). As you meet people gently greet them non-verbally and move on. Now stop in front of someone: explore their face. Allow a long time for this. Say goodbye non-verbally, move on. Continue with the same directions, and others: e.g. explore hands, play games with hands, be angry and fight with hands — now make up, explore backs, hair, etc. End with group hug in the centre.

**Variations**      See other blind games. Explore the room and allow inanimate objects in it.

C64  # Blind find

**Materials**    None (darkened room)

**Aims**    Trust building, fun, breaking down barriers, sensory
awareness.

**Procedure**    Darken room, everyone stand, (furniture pushed out of the
way), close eyes. Begin gently moving around, walking
slowly, no talking, when you meet people greet them non-
verbally, gently, and move on. Leader gives series of
instructions, gives plenty of time to experience each:

a   Find someone with hair the same length as yours. When you
find him take his hand and stand still. Someone else may join
you if his hair is also the same. After plenty of time, open
your eyes and check out your choice — is it really the same?

b   Find someone with feet as big as yours

c   Find someone with arms the same length as yours

d   Find someone with a nose like yours

e   Invent more things to find. (Clothes, mouths, hands.......)

C65          **Blindfold walking**

**Materials**    Blindfolds for half the group (optional)

**Aims**    Trust, concentration, self validation

**Procedure**    One person is blindfolded, or close eyes, the other gives
verbal instructions. The director is not allowed to touch the
directed. (Change roles). It is a good idea to use a chair as a
starting and a finishing point. Vary speeds. Obstacles placed
in areas and the process repeated.

**Variations**    1  Races between pairs can be given and times

2  Directions given by sounds only. i.e. one buzz for walk, two
buzzes for stop, etc. Try for variations of sound.

**Concentrative development**
Social development
Communication
Imagination, creativity


C66      **Bus**

**Materials**      None.  Chairs set up as bus, tall stool for the driver

**Aims**      Improvisation, role playing, fun, group interaction

**Procedure**      First practise 'riding' on bus, let someone be the driver, call
stops, make turns, etc. Passengers practise jolting along,
leaning for turns, lurching at stops, etc. Then have all
passengers adopt a role and maintain it, getting on and off
the bus, talking to the driver, passengers sitting next to them,
etc.  Suggest the roles if necessary:  lost old lady, man
carrying bags of smelly rubbish to the dump, woman in a
hurry, etc.  Begin developing incidents involving everyone,
such as hijacking, accident, drunks on bus, man wearing
monkey suit gets on bus, etc.

**Variations**      Have passengers introduce themselves in role, give autobiography.  Bus could be aeroplane.

C67        # Chain mime

**Materials**        None

**Aims**        Improve miming skills, concentration, memory training, fun

**Procedure**        Five people are chosen to leave the room — the group decides on a mime sequence for them to do, e.g. making a complicated sandwich, or changing a baby's nappy.

**a**  is called in and told what to do

**b**  is then called in and watches while **(a)** mimes changing the baby

**c**  is then called in, and **(b)** repeats what he saw **(a)** do.

**c**  repeats the mime for **(d)**, **(d)** repeats for **(e)**,

**e**  mimes it for the audience. (The usual result is that the mime changes with each repitition, so that **(e)** is doing something *entirely different*). Ask each person what he thought he was doing.

**Variations**        Have each person deliberately add something new

C68        # Chain statues

**Materials**    None

**Aims**    Warm-up for movement, trust building

**Procedure**    One person takes a statue position in the centre. Another comes up and moves an arm or leg or hand, etc. The leader may say 'freeze' at any point, and everyone stay exactly where he is. Continue until the whole group is up.

**Variations**    See other statue games

**Concentrative development**
Warm-up, ice-breaking
Relax, winding down
Communication, contact

C69      # Chinese whispers

**Materials**      None

**Aims**      Positive feedback, good for closing exercise

**Procedure**      Members mill around. When you see someone you'd like to communicate with, send them a message via someone else: e.g. 'Tell Joan I said thank you for helping me yesterday.' Continue until messages run out.

**Variations**      Do as graffiti on large paper on walls. Do with bits of paper being delivered. Do at a run, speed up, slow motion, etc.

C70          # Courtroom

**Materials**     None (set up room like a court)

**Aims**         Improvisation lead-up, imagination, group team work, fun

**Procedure**    Phase one: Choose barristers, lawyers, judge, etc. as well as
                plaintiff and defendant. Send all of these out of the room.
                Improvise plaintiff being robbed or attacked by defendant,
                arrested by policemen, in front of audience. Have plaintiff
                and defendant meet with their lawyers, and get witnesses
                from audience. Hold trial, as much according to real
                procedure as possible.

**Variations**   Invent new crimes, change roles, adapt for mime/movement

C71 **Comic strip**

**Materials**       None

**Aims**        Improvisation, group development

**Procedure**   Each group develops an improvisation around a theme of its
choice. When the improvisation is shown to the whole group,
however, it is shown as a series of tableaux as in comic strip
fashion.

Example       people on tube train

*Scene one:*   normal ride
*Scene two:*   train has lurched, passengers in disarray
*Scene three:* back to normal

**Variations**   1  Take a well known story and depict in a series of tableaux

2  Take a well known comic strip and parody it

Note        Limited conversation may be added, as long as there is no
movement about the scene.

C72    **Clockwork people**

**Materials**    None

**Aims**    Concentration, movement, improvisation

**Procedure**    Each person becomes a clockwork figure who goes through a complete performance when wound up. Leader should perhaps denote a particular length for the sequence which could be marked by suitable music. Emphasis should be given on starting and finishing points. Can be co-ordinated into Swiss clock, or group or robots, etc.

**Variations**    Develop so that action can be repeated exactly within a given time.

C73       # Comparisons & opposites

**Materials**       None

**Aims**       Improvisation, movement

**Procedure**       Work in pairs or teams: use mime or short improvisations

Compare       silence with noise, running with slow motion (really slow, almost imperceptible).
running and leaping with slow motion, exuberance with sorrow
old people — young people
tall people — short people
big (expansive and extrovert) — small (nervous and introvert)
floating — mud wallowing
sleek and darting — slow and ponderous
slow witted — quick witted
stiff person — loose person
rich — poor
strong — weak
industrious — lazy
taciturn person — chatterbox
Englishman — Frenchman
pompous person — friendly person
serious person — silly person
school teacher — school child
policeman — criminal
angel — devil
motorist — pedestrian
slow people — quick people

**Variations**       Development into improvisations: dealing with various situations; people might be involved in conversation, letter writing, shopping, etc.

C74     # Concentration points

**Materials**     Needs silence

**Aims**     Concentration, movement sensitivity

**Procedure**     The following are improvisations which can be done
individually or in whatever relationship is desired.

Following a pattern on the floor (real or imaginary):

stepping stones
carrying full cups or glasses
walking over ice
walking on a tightrope
walking along a ledge
walking through a minefield in the dark
climbing a rockface
unwrapping a parcel secretly
applying eye make-up/war paint
watching a suspense drama
getting a poisonous snake in a box
extend into improvisations
wrapping a gift
decorating a cake
defusing a bomb
building a card house
safebreaking
throwing a ball
smoke writing
stealing
getting into a cinema seat
tieing a tie
threading a needle
getting into a suit of paper tissue

C75     **Control yourself**

**Materials**     None

**Aims**     Trust, body control, sensory awareness

**Procedure**     The group is asked to lie down on their backs flat upon the floor, arms by their sides and their feet apart. Leader counts to ten (ten seconds approx.) during which time the group counts the number inhalations and exhalations (i.e. total breaths) they make, (average about 5); this amount is increased so that the group can count ten or higher breaths in ten seconds. The amount can also be reduced to one per second or one per twenty, etc.

**Variations**     1 Control the speed of walking in the group. Walking very quickly/suddenly, contrasted by infinitely slow pace.

2 Group lies on stomachs and each person arches backs using stomach as a balancing point. Feet and shoulders must leave the floor. Leader establishes the length of each 'stretch'.

3 Each person stands with arms by sides, feet slightly apart. Without the help of the leader each person allows himself to sway in any direction. The point being to sway to severe angles but not allowing any over-balancing.

C76        **Emotions**

**Materials**      None

**Aims**          Emotional awareness, values development

**Procedure**      Leader asks group to characterise particular feelings or
                emotions, i.e.:

pain            amusement       terror
pleasure        displeasure     fright
contempt        astonishment    loathing
weariness       indifference    degradation
honour          triumph         alarm
fear            loss            worry
hatred          excitement      shame
impatience      relief

These emotions may be shown in a statue pose or moving or
walking around. Sometimes it is good to include movement
which the leader can freeze at will.

**Variations**     After striking a statue pose to represent a particular emotion
                the person is given six beats of a drum etc. to change fully
                into a different emotional stance.

Inter-relate with other emotions

C77          # Face touch

**Materials**     None

**Aims**         Trust building, sensory awareness, easy lead-in to group
feeling. Best in group of 20 or more.

**Procedure**    Divide group into A's and B's. A's sit down in scattered
chairs, close eyes. No talking at all. Each B sits beside an A,
places A's hands on B's shoulders. A explores B's face, hair,
hands and shoulders. (Optional: A says positive sentences
starting: 'Now I am aware.......' e.g. 'Now I am aware that
your hair is soft, etc.') After a time, B stands and goes to
join the rest of B's in a line. A now opens eyes and goes to
find his partner in the line. A tells B how he identified him
in the line. Switch roles and repeat.

C78     **Finish the action**

**Materials**     None

**Aims**     Improve mime skills, group interaction, imagination, lead up to improvisation.

**Procedure**     One person begins to mime an action: e.g. surgeon operating on a patient. As soon as it is clear what he is doing, another (perhaps eventually the whole group) joins in: **non-verbal**. Continue until a natural ending is reached. Try to motivate the group to avoid easy/violent options for endings: e.g. blowing up the operating room.

**Variations**     Add words, sounds

C79            **Fit the reader**

**Materials**      A magazine, newspaper or book

**Aims**          Imagination, fun, drama situations

**Procedure**   1  The leader chooses a piece of written material. Any
                   paragraph, ordinary or otherwise.

                2  He explains how each person in the group is to assume the
                   role of a particular *kind* of reader.

                3  The person is given the paragraph to read — without
                   preparation — in the manner or style chosen by the reader.

Examples           in the manner of a horse racing commentator as the horses
                   near the post.

                   in the manner of a children's story reader

                   in a style of a dignitary making a speech on a public
                   occasion.

                   in a style full of insinuation and innuendo

                   in the style of a church minister or priest

                   in the manner of a suspicious policeman

C80      # Fun fair

**Materials**      None

**Aims**      Improvisation, group development

**Procedure**      While group is split into half, then each half splits into
smaller groups and develop different sideshows at a fun fair.
When complete, one half act as members of the public who
are visiting the fair while the other half try to attract people
to their sideshows and let the people have a go. This
situation is later evened so that the other side become the
fair ground people.

Ideas for
sideshows
Shooting gallery
Boxing display (have a go)
Wall of Death
Swings
Darts
Roundabouts
One-armed bandits (fruit machines)
Candy, toffee apples, etc.
Coits
The amazing ........
Wrestling
Juggling
For sale
Bingo

**Variations**      1   Develop the theme of 'The amazing........' Each exhibit
having something different and amazing to show.

2   Do silently, develop into movement

C81    # Gibberish

**Materials**    None

**Aims**    Trust, personal development, expression

**Procedure**    The leader splits the group into pairs and suggests the point of a forthcoming conversation. It is then explained that no recognisable words will be used. The pair will talk as if in a foreign language, making up words and sounds. The point of the exercise is to develop in intensity of expression excluding real words.

*Ideas for conversation*

1  Lend me some money

2  Where were you last night?

3  Go home, your house has been burgled

4  It was the funniest game I've seen

5  Did you see that T.V. programme last night?

6  You've been brought here to talk and you'll tell us all we want to know.

**Variations**    Instead of sounds, or new words, numbers can be used

C82     **Group statues**

**Materials**     None

**Aims**     Warm up for movement, trust building

**Procedure**     Sit in a circle on the floor. One person takes a statue-like
position in the centre. The group names the statue. Another
person joins him, relating his own position to the original
statue. Give the new statue a name. Continue until the
group statue seems complete.

**Variations**     See other statue games

C83 **Guillotine**

**Materials**    Pencil and paper

**Aims**    Lead up to improvisation

**Procedure**    Partners decide on and write down six lines of conversation (three lines each). Use this as script. Now change the situation and repeat the same lines:

a  as if crossing the Sahara Desert

b  as if taking a man to the guillotine

c  as if you were two newlyweds at breakfast

d  any situation of your own choosing

C84     # Impersonations

**Materials**     None

**Aims**     Improvisation, characterisation, group development

**Procedure**     Discuss what a parody entails. Each group decides which T.V. programme they are going to parody and spends about half an hour preparing their work. It is important that this is done properly and that when the groups show their work they are concerned with achieving humour through parody and not through other means. The group leader should help each group in its preparation where help is wanted and each parody must have a set length of time, i.e. 5 — 10 mins.

**Variations**    1   Famous sportsmen

              2   Politicians

              3   Local figures

C85          # Indian teepee

**Materials**      None

**Aims**         Concentration, fun, develop non-verbal expression

**Procedure**     Sit in a circle on the floor, each member chooses an Indian
name and a non-verbal sign to go with it. (e.g. Falling Rain —
ripple fingers in the air; Sleeping Papoose — close eyes, rock
baby, etc.) From now on it is non-verbal. One member
starts, makes his sign and someone else's. Whoever has the
sign he's made, must respond immediately with that sign (his
own) and someone else's, etc. If he doesn't respond
immediately, he's out, and moves back out of the circle. The
game should go very quickly. When only two are left, they
try to get each other out.

**Variations**     Shout name while doing sign. Throw an object to the person
whose sign you are making. Send other person's sign only,
omitting your own.

C86 **Inside out**

**Materials**    None

**Aims**    Developing imagination, self-validation, sensory awareness, awareness, body control.

**Procedure**    Whole group lies on backs, arms on the floor, legs separate, eyes closed. Leader talks smoothly and steadily and asks the group to focus their senses within their bodies. Bodies are described as containing blood vessels with blood pulsing through; lungs exchanging oxygen for carbon dioxide (good air for used air); stomachs digesting food, etc. Group is asked to concentrate on one particular function of the body and the leader asks the group to be aware (even synthetically) of the existence of the activity, without feeling for signs with their hands.

*'Real' sensations to notice*
heartbeat
pulse
breathing
indigestion
digestion
perspiration, etc.

*'Pseudo' sensations (to imagine entirely)*
hair growing
nails growing
air in the blood
food passing to muscles
acids attacking the teeth, etc.

**Variations**    1 Concentration through breathing. Take a deep breath. Imagine your ribs expanding, the air rushing down your throat, filling your lungs, entering your blood and kicking the old air out. (continue with exhaling.)

2 Concentration through heartbeat. Blood sucked into one chamber — expelled into next chamber and then back into vein or artery. Concentration upon the feeling (in rhythm with the beats) of this expansion and contraction.

C87 **Killer**

**Materials**     Card pack

**Aims**          Concentration, eye contact, fun

**Procedure**     Sit in a circle, pass a card to each player, who peeks at it
and keeps it hidden. Watch each other. Queen of Spades is
the 'KILLER'. If he winks at you, you wait a few seconds,
throw your card in the centre and say, 'I'm dead'. Do not
tell who killed you. (Once you're dead, you can say nothing.)
If you think you know the Killer, say, 'I accuse........' If
you're wrong, you throw you card in: you have committed
Suicide. Game ends when the Killer is discovered.

C88     **Look closer**

**Materials**     Each person to have some ordinary object out, such as a pen, pencil, etc.

**Aims**     To sharpen sensitivity and awareness and discover the uniqueness of everyday items.

**Procedure**     Each person examines a small object, usually in everyday use, something simple like a pencil. Look it over very carefully and examine it closely. Then notice the over-all shape, any scratches, blemishes, any design or pattern; the leader tells his group to repeat the name of the object silently.

See if the name of the object seems inadequate

'Become the object': experience or try to describe what it is like to be that thing.

Introduce yourself to others

**Concentrative development**
Movement, body skills
Warm-up, ice-breaking
Relax, winding-down

C89

# Magic drum

**Materials**    Drum and beater

**Aims**    Loosening-up, warming-up for movement

**Procedure**    Leader says: This is a magic drum, you can only move when you hear it beating. (beats) Move ..... freeze. (Repeat until they all freeze immediately at the stop of the drum beat.) Now the magic drum is even stronger, and you must move with the beat of the drum, but you must also move the way I tell you.

**Be**    spiky
jerky
smooth
faster
slower
old
young
melting like warm butter, etc.

**Variations**    Use piano or other rhythm instruments. Let a student use the drum.

C90 **Machines 1**

**Materials**     None

**Aims**         Concentration, group development

**Procedure**     One member of the group moves into a space and begins a machine-like movement. Each other member of the group joins the activity and 'develops' the machine. This can be done by linking in some way to the *action* of any of the people already in the machine. Music can be particularly helpful in this activity or each person could make a different sound for his action.

**Variations**    1 Machine could be joined into total group

2 Leader can choose machine tasks for groups

C91 **Machines 2**

**Materials**     None

**Aims**     Lead up to improvisation or movement, group decision-making, fun.

**Procedure**     Divide into groups of 4 to 7 people, use the people to create a machine with moving parts. See that each person in the group is involved, either as part of the machine or operating it or being a product of it, etc. Show the machine to other groups.

**Variations**     1  add noises

2  assign a specific machine:

2.1  voodoo curse machine
2.2  laugh machine
2.3  juke box
2.4  trouble-making machine
2.5  insult machine

3  make a human development machine or a joy machine.

4  make a factory, using the large group

5  make a machine to suit purposes of group, e.g. primary education machine, etc.

C92 **The Mirror**

**Materials** None (large empty space)

**Aims** Concentration, silence, group togetherness, drama warm-ups, mime training, learning to observe.

**Procedure** (First time). Stand in circle, watch leader, leader moves *very slowly,* using first just hands, then other parts of body and face. *Others move with him as in a mirror.* Stress slowness (raise hand to shoulder height on count of ten). Stress staying together. Illustrate difference between mirroring and following.

**Variations** Do in pairs: watch partner's eyes while mirroring. Turn back on partner, listen to breathing, sense when partner is turning around, mirror the turn and movement. Work for total concentration. Take turns leading and mirroring, pass the leadership back and forth.

Give specific situations to mirror in two pairs.

Examples barber and customer
milliner and customer
dress saleslady and customer

Sound mirror watch partner's face closely,
mirror sounds.

C93 **Notice a colour**

**Materials** None

**Aims** Sensory development

**Procedure** Choose one particular colour and notice that colour and all of its shades during the rest of the day. See how many shades you can give a name to.

Invent names

Choose a different colour and compare results with original colour.

Notice colour combinations. Look closely to see how many different colours go together and merge to make the overall shade. Check everyday items such as apples, book covers, etc. See how many colours are there. If you have chance, check an oil painting for the same qualities.

**Variations** In group, place pieces of coloured paper on the floor. Each person chooses one, examines the colour, concentrates on it, 'becomes' that colour.

Write poetry or improvise around it.

C94          **Orchestration**

**Materials**      None

**Aims**       Concentration, group development

**Procedure**    Each member of the group decides upon one particular
method of producing a sound. Each person's sound should be
different from the next person's, etc. The main directive is
that it should be possible to produce the sound at will, and
also vary its strength. The leader then canvasses for a well
known rhythm of a particular tune and starts the group
humming the tune in unison. The leader then asks each
person in turn to continue the tune using their own
particular sound. It is up to the leader to decide whether
or not this is a totally individual effort, or whether the
background music continues. After each person has 'played'
once, the whole group 'orchestrates' the tune — every person
using their own individual sound at once. Leader can mimic
a real conductor by emphasising some sounds and reducing
others.

**Variations**    Invent own tunes.

Work in groups amplifing or balancing sounds for a better
effect.

C95      # Paper bag dramatics

**Materials**

Characters written on cards (e.g. doctor, lift operator, bricklayer, etc.) and divided up with seven or eight in a bag.

**Aims**

Lead up to improvisation, group interaction, fun, imagination.

**Procedure**

Small groups, each one has a bag of characters, must use characters to create a scene. Share and evaluate scenes.

**Variations**

Combine with prop-building or proverb-building.

C96

# Pass the object

**Materials**     None

**Aims**     Concentration, mime, fun

**Procedure**     Sit in a circle. Leader holds imaginary object, e.g. egg beater, and mimes using it for its purpose. He then passes it on to the next person, who 'uses' it, and then by making a rubbing motion with his hands, erases it and substitutes a new imaginary object, e.g. an ice-cream cone. Continue around the circle.

**Variations**     Leader 'uses' object, second person uses that one plus another, adding all the way around the circle — this would make It a memory game.

**Concentrative development**
Trust, group interaction
Focal, concentration
Introductory, ice-breaker
Drama training

C97        **Pass the sound**

**Materials**      None

**Aims**      Sensory awareness, building feeling of group, concentration

**Procedure**      Stand in a circle, arms around each other (optional), close
eyes. Leader starts by making any sound (e.g. click tongue,
hum, etc.). Next person makes a sound of his own. Try
speeding up, slowing down, all at once, etc.

**Variations**      Spread out and hide around the room, experiment with
random sounds.

Try atmospheric sounds: sounds of forest, ocean, outer
space, farm.

Make a sound for every single movement or action; arm-
raising sound, jump-sound, etc.

C98        # Photographers & models

**Materials**   None

**Aims**        Concentration, self-validation

**Procedure**   Photographers place the person, including their features into a pose that they feel representative of that person. Leader must explain how artists and photographers try to capture their models' personality and character in a pose. Models can resist.

**Variations**  Models decide how they would like to move. Photographers or models decide on the people they would like to be, or would like to copy.

C99 **Picture**

**Materials** Pack of pictures

**Aims** Improvisation, role-playing, social development and identity awareness, etc.

**Procedure** Leader shows picture or series of pictures on one particular theme. The group discuss the implications seen in the scenes and develop an improvisation based on the theme discussed.

**Variations** Develop a similar situation by presenting smaller groups with a picture each.

Note in this activity more ideas should be drawn from the group than should be given by the leader.

C100 **Polarities**

**Materials**      None

**Aims**          Concentration, movement

**Procedure**     Group acts out individual responses to contrasting forms, e.g.

spiky, *smooth*
angry, *placid*
heavy, *light*
small, *tall*
swamp creature, *drifting/floating creature/sky diver*
small moon, *huge planet*

*Leader can add own ideas*

**Variations**    1  In six beats of the drum grow from one form to its
contrasting opposite. (each polarity is a 'freeze' from a
statue).

2  Polarities are personified into people showing those
personality trends. Improvisations can be built on these,
working perhaps in pairs.

C101        **Prop building**

**Materials**      Props, assorted

**Aims**           Lead up to improvisation, overcome shyness

**Procedure**      Divide into small groups, each group is given a prop, around
                   which to build a scene; e.g. an alarm clock, a treasure, a
                   telephone, etc.  Share scenes and evaluate.

**Variations**     Give several props to each group, which must all be
                   incorporated in the scene.

                   Keep same prop, but change scene.

**Concentrative development**
Drama training
Imagination, — creativity
Movement, body skills
Warm-up, ice-breakers

C102        **Proverbs**

**Materials**        None

**Aims**        Improvisation, communication, group interaction

**Procedure**        Each group is given one proverb as a starter for a timed
improvisation (or brainstorm your own). Leader should
discuss interpretation with each group beforehand.
Improvisation can be literal or developed in a symbolic
way; also in a mime or verbally.

A bird in the hand is worth two in the bush
A drowning man will clutch at a stone
A friend in need is a friend indeed
A rolling stone gathers no moss
A stitch in time saves nine
Absence makes the heart grow fonder
Actions speak louder than words
All that glitters is not gold
All's fair in love and war
Better late than never
Birds of a feather flock together
Blood is thicker than water
Charity begins at home
Discretion is the better part of valour
Don't put all your eggs in one basket
Don't count your chickens before they're hatched
Don't tell tales out of school
Empty vessels make the most noise
Every cloud has a silver lining
Forewarned is forearmed
It's an ill wind that blows nobody any good
It never rains but it pours
Look before you leap
Make hay while the sun shines
Many hands make light work
Necessity is the mother of invention

**Variations**        1   Are all proverbs true? Show

2   Can you think of any conflicting proverbs? Show

3   What or why proberbs? What purpose? Discuss

4   Make your own. Show

| C103 | # Remember |
|------|-----------|

**Materials**    None

**Aims**    Concentration, memory

**Procedure**    Everyone studies the room and the people in it. One person goes out and the group changes something or someone. 'It' must come back in and try to find out what's changed.

**Variations**

1 Add something instead

2 Do in pairs, study each other, turn backs, change something.

**Concentrative development**

Drama training
Introductory
Warm-up, ice-breaker
Movement, body skills

C104    # Sentence themes

**Materials**    None

**Aims**    Improvisation, characterisation, social development

**Procedure**    Each group is given one sentence theme as a starter for a timed improvisation. The sentence must be used by one of the characters in the play either as opening or closing line.

'Pass the salt'
'I wonder if I dare ask my boss for a rise?'
'He loses his temper so easily'
'Nobody in this house ever listens to me'
'Why can't you get home on time?'
'I don't want you out on the streets after dark'
'I spent the whole afternoon cooking dinner and none of you have eaten a thing'
'Hey, darling, I've some bad news for you'
'I've been hearing things about you'
'I always knew that would happen'

**Variations**    Develop into class drama: examine motives, etc. Combine some sentences. Brainstorm opening sentences. Explore the idea that without conflict or a problem there is no drama.

C105        **Silence is fragile**

**Materials**        Space and silence

**Aims**        Sensory awareness, self-validation, concentration

**Procedure**    1   Each member of the group (a) lies down on the floor with eyes closed.
or (b) sits crosslegged with eyes closed.

2   Leader asks for complete silence, and no contact between people

3   The group is then asked quietly to notice how calm and quiet everything is.

4   Each person then has to *think* of a particular exclamation (such as a scream) which would tear this silence in two.

5   After a minute the leader explains how he will touch each person in turn and as soon as they feel this touch they literally leap out across the room uttering the cry and return just as suddenly to their silent pose wherever they 'land'.

6   The leader must wait for complete calm before touching the next person.

C106                **Silent movies**

**Materials**          None

**Aims**               Concentration, improvisation, group development, develop-
                       ment of basic elements.

**Procedure**          This type of improvisation can be used as either a starter or
                       as a development of another improvisation. The point is to
                       exaggerate the action involved with the improvisation and
                       ideally to reduce complicated ideas into basic themes.

                       Improvisation must be 'shown' to effect with simplicity of
                       form.  Any theme can be used.

Examples               Parodies of various manner of film and plays, i.e. spies,
                       romantic, thrillers, 40s movies, etc.

**Concentrative development**
Drama training
Movement, body skills
Introductory
Warm-up, ice-breaker

C107 **Situation**

**Materials** None. (Could have situations painted on cards)

**Aims** Lead up to drama, improvisation

**Procedure** Divide in small groups, give each group a situation, e.g. waiting in a maternity ward, trapped in an elevator, etc. Show improvisations one by one. Then take the same situations, change the characters involved and repeat. Share scenes and evaluate.

**Variations** Trade situations among groups. Let each group do the same situation but with different characters.

C108     # Sound detectives

**Materials**     Pencil and paper

**Aims**     Memory training, concentration, sensory awareness

**Procedure**     Lead up: close your eyes and listen. What's the nearest sound you can hear? The loudest? The softest? The farthest away? Now the leader walks softly around the room, making a series of sounds, about five to start with, (e.g. click a scissor, leaf through a book, etc.) Members open eyes and list the sounds they heard, in order. Check them and discuss the experience.

**Variations**     Keep lengthening the list of sounds, make weird and unidentifiable sounds. Let pupils take turns making sounds.

**Concentrative development**
Movement, body skills
Introductory
Drama training
Trust, group interaction

C109      **Statues**

**Materials**      None

**Aims**      Warm up for movement or drama, trust building

**Procedure**      Choose partners, designate A and B. A stands still but relaxed, B moulds him, as though he were a lump of clay, in into a statue. When you are finished, walk around and look at the other statues. If you see something you'd like to change, change it. Return to your own statue and decide whether to leave it as it is, or change or restore it. Give it a name. Share names or ideas aloud. Switch and repeat.

**Variations**      See other statue games

C110     # Statue groups

**Materials**     None. A tambour or drum can be used however

**Aims**     Concentration, group development

**Procedure**     Group works out a statuary tableau

Ideas

| from history | family life |
|---|---|
| mythology | school life |
| television | hospital |
| films | etc. etc. |
| famous stories | |
| great inventors | |

**Variations**     Each group viewed by others in turn. After each group has been viewed by the other groups, the tableau can be incorporated into an improvisation. The improvisation can begin from the tableau or end with the tableau. Set a time limit on each improvisation.

C111      # Still pond

**Materials**      One blindfold

**Aims**      Trust building, sensory awareness

**Procedure**      Blindfolded person in the centre. Everyone else moves around until he says, 'Still Pond'. He moves forward and explores a face, guesses who it is. If he guesses, takes off blindfold, if not, he tries again.

**Variations**      As he moves forward, people make music or noises, while he searches for a specific person. (He might say 'I'm going to find David, etc.')

C112     # Story wheel

**Materials**     None

**Aims**     Imagination, build group feeling

**Procedure**     Group lies down on their backs in wheel formation, heads to the centre, one person starts story, next one continues, etc. Try to create mood or atmosphere to fit story.

**Variations**     Sit in circle, have storyteller walk around and act out story before passing it on.

C113      # Toyshop

**Materials**      Darkened room, lighting or candles, piano or other music, —
optional.

**Aims**      Improvisation, discovery of talent, movement, fun, — adults
enjoy this as much as children.

**Procedure**      Brainstorm kinds of toys which move. Become various toys
and move around room. Stop, start, and trade toys (roles).
Choose roles for the improvisation: toymaker, two robbers,
policeman, toy soldiers, other toys. Leader tells story, group
acts it out. Story in brief: an old toymaker tries out his toys,
then locks up the shop and goes home. The toys come alive
at midnight and play. Two robbers steal into the shop,
seeking the toymaker's savings. As they are about to find the
money, toy soldiers come in, capture and tie them up; in the
morning, toymaker returns, finds robbers, calls policeman.
He will never know who captured the robbers.

**Variations**      Have students invent new toys, new story.

*Other directed improvisations:*
wax museum
art gallery
clock shop
history museum
department store at midnight
200

C114     # Travel agent

**Materials**     None

**Aims**     Improvisation, imagination, fun

**Procedure**     Divide into groups of 3 — 4. Choose roles, travel agent and types of customers. Develop roles by asking for ages, sexes, types, problems, of customers and agents. Improvise plays in travel bureau, which could include time travel, space travel, etc. Share improvisations. Evaluate.

**Variations**     Do as a whole group

C115      # Treasure chest

**Materials**      4 or 5 chosen objects

**Aims**      Develop imagination, improvisation

**Procedure**      Leader shows four or five objects separately to the whole group. Each object is discussed as to its possible or projected uses. Members of the group can step forward and show how the object could be used. (This both clarifies use and after use allows individual development of ideas). Eventually group is split into small groups and each group is given an object around which to build an improvisation. The improvisation may be shown afterwards.

Ideas for objects      long broom handle (spear, etc.)
large piece of plain cloth
simulated parchment (map)
large plastic ring
a heavy key
old transistor radio
cardboard/paper tube
handkerchief (with initial)
decorated goblet or crown
empty film canister

**Variations**      Individuals try to auction the objects which are shown.

C116    **Vibrations**

**Materials**    None

**Aims**    Self-validation, inter-personal development

**Procedure**    In pairs:

a   Bring your two hands close to your partner's two hands, (palm to palm) until they are almost touching.

b   Close eyes and experience the sensation of warmth or energy

c   Experiment with distances

**Variations**    1   Try blindfold — discuss effect

2   Use faces instead of palms

3   Do in a circle.

C117 **Wax museum**

**Materials**      None (costumes, optional)

**Aims**          Improvisation, concentration, imagination, fun

**Procedure**     Brainstorm famous figures to appear in wax museum, some
in groups. Try being the still figures, add costume if desired.
Have students invent story about wax museum, e.g. sculptor
uses real people for figures, etc. Improvise the story.

**Variations**    Change story

## C118          What can you feel?

**Materials**      None

**Aims**          Sensory development, concentration

**Procedure**     Each person is asked to notice particularly the textures they
can feel. In this activity the leader must classify the groups'
surroundings in such a way that they can report small groups
of objects noted particularly. Each person or small group
may be given separate classifications to seek out, or the
group as a whole may be set each classification in turn.
Group may suggest its own classification.

Ideas for classification

| rough | turns | sticky | hard |
|-------|-------|--------|------|
| smooth | splintery | wet | prickly |
| sharp | gritty | dry | spongy |
| cold | woven | delicate | squelchy |
| cool | soft | silky | sturdy |
| warm | coarse | scratched | hot |
| crumbly | etc. | | |

Discuss afterwards why they include particular objects in
their classifications.

**Variations**    1  Compare interior textures with exerior ones

2  Run to each article when it is named.

3  Pass objects around for blindfolded experience.

C119      # What can you hear?

**Materials**      None

**Aims**      Sensory development, concentration

**Procedure**      Whole group either:

or

**a** lie down on the floor with eyes closed
**b** sit crosslegged with eyes closed.

Leader asks for *complete* silence and stresses there be no contact during the time set. During this time each person listens very carefully and counts and remembers every single sound they can hear. At the end of the activity each member lists the things that they heard — or a list is compiled from the class as a whole.

Discuss which sounds are most audible, and likes and dislikes, etc.

**Variations**      Compare the sounds of an interior room with the sounds outside the building.

C120      # What can you see?

**Materials**      None

**Aims**      Sensory development, concentration

**Procedure**      Each person is asked to notice particularly the things they can see. In this activity the leader must classify the group's surroundings in such a way that they can report small groups of objects noted particularly. Each person or small group may be given a separate classification to seek out, or the group as a whole may be set and asked to classify in turn. Group may suggest classification.

Ideas for classifications (each may be going through intermediary classification, too.)

distant, *near*
huge, *tiny*
reds, blues, yellows, *tones, etc.*
colourful, *drab*
horizontal, *vertical*
straight, *rounded*
even, *uneven*
delicate, *sturdy*
shiny, *dull*
light, *dark*
outstanding, *obscure*
natural, *artificial*
plain, *patterned*
interesting, *boring*

discussion afterwards on why they chose particular classifications.

**Variations**      1   Compare the abundance of one classification inside or outside

2   Run to each article when it is named.

C121     **What is it?**

**Materials**

One chair for each group

**Aims**

Improvisation

**Procedure**

Each group takes one inanimate object such as a chair, or a
broom, etc., and each person uses it in a different way, i.e.
a chair could become a wheelbarrow, a horse, a crate, a
sleigh, etc. etc. Try to develop as many strange uses as
possible.

**Variations**

More than one person may be used to demonstrate a
particular use.

C122     # Who am I?

**Materials**     None

**Aims**     Improvisation; imagination

**Procedure**     **a** Each person chooses to become a famous character either from history, entertainment, literature, government, etc.

**b** Leader asks each person to sit separately and concentrate on:

b1   the kind of personality the character has.

b2   their mannerisms.

b3   the way they talk.

b4   what they say.

**c** When everyone is ready they can stand up as the character they have chosen and move around an introduce themselves to each other.

**d** They can also hold conversations with one another making sure they retain all the characteristics of the famous person.

C123          # Who started the motion?

**Materials**     None

**Aims**          Concentration, trust building

**Procedure**     Circle; one person (A) leaves. Leader chooses someone to
start the motions such as slapping, tapping feet, waving, etc.
Everyone watches the starter and changes motions when he
does, while appearing not to watch him. 'A' has to guess who
the starter is.

**Variations**    Use blindfold and change sounds instead of motions.

# Introductory games

## Contents

I124        **Famous people**

**Materials**     Famous names on strips of card or paper, straight pins. Could
be real people (Joan of Arc), fictional (Superman), etc.

**Aims**          Mixing, starting conversation, ice-breaking

**Procedure**     As people enter, leader pins a name on each person's back.
Each one must walk around and try to find out who he is
by asking yes-or-no questions of everyone else. When he
knows who he is, he pins the paper on his front and
continues to help others.

**Variations**    Try it non-verbally. Try insisting that everyone must make
statements (e.g. 'I am alive'), and no questions allowed.

I125     # Getting to know you

**Materials**     None

**Aims**     Introduction, memorizing names

**Procedure**     Whole group is spread over area. At a given signal they must move around and shake hands with as many people as possible. With every handshake they are introducing themselves; each person should try to remember as many names as possible. The leader must make every effort to establish a *real* introduction and not an empty one.

I126       **Group fantasy trip**

**Materials**   None

**Aims**        Relexation, build group feeling, inspire creativity, imagination

**Procedure**   Stretch out comfortably, close eyes, concentrate on breathing. Let imagination roam. When an image comes clearly to mind, speak out and describe it. Others listen, feel free to add to images, without interrupting. Continue as long as it seems rewarding, allowing long silences when they develop.

**Variations**  Add soft music. Draw or paint images as they occur. Dance or improvise fantasies. Do gentle massage during fantasies.

I127 **Move to the spot**

**Materials**      Large, empty room or space

**Aims**        Learning to follow simple instructions, movement, warm-up
             for Drama

**Procedure**   Leader says: 'Find a place to stand by yourself. Now look at
             and concentrate on a fixed spot on the floor, somewhere
             across the room. Now, move to that spot in a straight line,
             pacing yourself so as not to have to stop, while avoiding
             bumping into anyone.'

             Leader continues to give similar instructions, allowing time fo
             individuals to (A) concentrate on each spot, (B) move at thei
             own pace, and (C) settle into the new spot.

             Instructions for (B) could include moving to the new spot:

             1    backwards
             2    in as few steps as possible
             3    in as many steps as possible
             4    travelling in circles
             5    travelling in squares
             6    using as few jumps as possible
             7    with hands on knees, toes etc.
             8    moving along floor without using hands
             9    with a partner, using only two out of four legs
             10   reflecting various emotions, e.g., fear, etc.

**Variations**   Have group invent more instructions.

I128        # How do you like your neighbour?

**Materials**        Chairs

**Aims**        Exercise, warm-ups, fun

**Procedure**        Chairs in a circle. Number each person, 1, 2, 3, 4 etc. One person in centre, remove one chair. The centre person points to someone and says 'How Do You Like Your Neighbour?'

There are two ways to answer:

**a**  *'I like him'.* In this case, everyone gets up and moves to another chair. Last one standing is in the centre next.

**b**  *'I don't like him'.* In this case, centre person asks 'Who do you want?'. The answerer calls any two numbers — the two people on his right and left must move, and the two people with the numbers called must try to get their chairs.

b2 When asked 'Who do you want?', the answerer says: 'Nobody', then everyone *except* the answerer runs around the outside of the circle, until the answerer says 'Stop'. Everyone then goes for a chair.

**Variations**        Invent new answers with the group

I129

# Human noughts & crosses (Tic-Tac-Toe)

**Materials**     9 chairs, running space

**Aims**          Active participation, warm-up, fun

**Procedure**     At one end of the room, three rows of three chairs each, fou
feet apart. Teams: Team 1 is 'Noughts', Team 2 is 'Crosses
they line up in corners of the room facing the chairs. When
the leader calls 'noughts', the first nought runs to a chair anc
sits with arms circled above head. Runner must sit before
Leader counts to 5 slowly. Leader calls 'crosses', first cross
runs and sits with arms crossed on chest. Leader continues t
call them alternately until one team wins (same rules as
paper Noughts and Crosses). Start over, call losing team firs
Keep score (optional).

**Variations**    For more active warm-up, do outside with long running
space.

I130      **Identifipicture**

**Materials**      None

**Aims**      Indentity. Warm-up

**Procedure**      One person in the group stands with their back to the group
and another person describes someone in the group. They
must be careful to describe each person in a positive way, and
not in a fashion which could be seen as derogatory. There is a
time allowance during which the person has to guess who is
being described. The person out front has then to choose
another person to come out front and the former then
chooses someone else to describe.

**Variations**      The person at the front asks questions instead of just giving
answers.

I131          # Man the ship

**Materials**      None — large room

**Aims**           Warm-up, exercises, fun, concentration

**Procedure**      Group forms one line (single file) down the centre of the
room. If the Leader shouts, 'Man the Starboard' — everyone
runs right. If the Leader shouts, 'Man the Port' — everyone
runs left. 'Man the Ship' means back to the centre. Leader
shouts commands faster and faster: last person to arrive at
any line is out. Eliminate until one person wins.

I132          # Mill & grab

**Materials**    None

**Aims**         Form groups, mix people, be active

**Procedure**    Mill around. Leader calls number (e.g. '5'), members run to
made circles of 5, holding hands up together. Those left over
go to one spot, perhaps can form another group. Leader
waits until all the groups are ready, then calls another
number, e.g. '2', '25', etc. (If the leader wants groups of 7
for the next game, he stops with 7, tells groups to keep their
7 and sit down). Exphasize that groups must be mixed, boys
and girls, teachers and pupils, etc.

**Variations**   Do with eyes closed. Do in silence. Do in slow motion. Do as
noisily as possible. Do according to an adverb, e.g. childishly,
etc.

I133            # The name of the game

**Materials**       One ball for every group of about 15 — 16.

**Aims**            Introduction, memorizing names

**Procedure**       New group sits in a circle of not more than sixteen. One
                person is given a ball. The ball is passed around the circle
                and each person who receives the ball says their name very
                clearly (usually just the first name). When everyone has been
                named and the ball is back to the beginning, the person
                holding the ball throws it to any person. That person must
                say the thrower's name. The ball is then thrown to someone
                else who must say the next thrower's name. If a person
                cannot remember the name of the person who has thrown
                the ball to him, they must ask and repeat the name before
                proceeding with the activity. The game continues until
                everyone can remember the names of the people within their
                group. Group size is usually about sixteen.

I134  **Persuasion**

**Materials**  Chocolate bars (about one for every five people), or any similar prize.

**Aims**  Test imagination and powers of persuasion

**Procedure**  Select three judges, give them time to design a points system. Each student comes before the judges, one by one, and tries to convince them that he should deserve a chocolate bar. Points should be awarded for originality and persuasiveness.

**Variations**  Do in writing; make an improvisation where the judges are bribed, etc.

I135      **Sherlock Holmes**

**Materials**      Items in possession, pencil and paper

**Aims**      Get acquainted, trust building

**Procedure**      Take six items from handbag, person, or pocket, show them to your partner. Do not talk. Write down what you have deduced about your partner from looking at his belongings. Share your deductions with the group, and get a response from your partner as to how accurate they are.

**Variations**      Put everyone's items on a table — decide what belongs to whom, and why.

I136     **Simon says**

**Materials**     None

**Aims**     Concentration, fun

**Procedure**     Each group chooses a leader who leads by performing actions to be imitated by the rest of the group, before each section the leader says:

*'Simon says* — Put your hands on your head'.

If the leader gives any order without the prefix 'Simon says', the group should not imitate the action or follow the order. If any member makes a mistake he leaves the group until the end of the activity. This activity is better if speed is emphasised.

**Variations**    1   Change leaders

             2   Think of ways to make it more difficult.

I137      **Squeeze & stretch**

**Materials**      None

**Aims**      Relaxation, body control, sensory awareness

**Procedure**      Each person sits on the floor with their knees drawn up, arms are clasped tightly around their legs, heads buried in their knees, back arched tightly; calves, thighs, buttocks, neck, fists, feet, — all clenched: shoulders forward and around legs, face muscles tightened — every muscle contracted and tightened. Hold that position for at least a minute and then very slowly release and unwind until your body is really spread and relaxed. Then each person immediately progresses to a stretching position when toes and fingers are spread, back arched, legs and arms extended fully, all joints are pulled apart (mention in turn, ankles, elbows, etc.): face is opened with wide eyes, tongue out, etc.

Now relax fully.

Discuss afterwards the awareness of tension. By deliberately creating tension and then relaxing, you can often alleviate tension received from outside sources.

I138        **Tangle**

**Materials**    None

**Aims**    Group development, trust, warm-up

**Procedure**    Whole group links hands into a human chain. First person
leads chain through itself, over and under arms, between
legs, etc. Extra care must be taken not to break the chain, to
move slowly and to be gentle. Tangle ends when group is too
tightly packed to move. One person then untangles the
group, giving them directions without touching them.

I139        **Tick tock**

**Materials**    Two small different objects, such as a blue felt pen and a red
felt pen.

**Aims**    Breaking the ice, concentration

**Procedure**    Leader has pen (or other object), passes it to his right,
saying: 'This is a tick'. Player 1 says: 'A what?' Leader
repeats: 'A tick'. 1 then passes it on saying, 'This is a tick'.
Player 2 says: 'A what?' to player 1, who says: 'A what?' to
the leader. Each time the 'What?' must pass all the way to
the leader, and the 'A tick' must pass all the way back,
before the pen is passed. When this has been practised a few
times, start over, and at the same time, start another pen to
the left, saying: 'This is a tock', etc. Confusion is
encouraged and acceptable. Let the group try, as long as
desired, to return both objects to the leader without losing
the flow or concentration.

## I140    Two-minute autobiographies

**Materials**    None

**Aims**    Mixing, self-awareness, self-disclosure, trust building.

**Procedure**    Find a partner, preferably one you don't know at all. You have two minutes to tell them what you would especially like them to know about you and your life:  past, present, hopes, plans, facts, etc.  After each has a turn, join another pair, and introduce your partner to them, telling what you remember about their autobiography.  When each of the four has had a turn, join the whole group and introduce your partner to them.  Do a round of 'I learned'.

**Variations**    Stop with either the pairs or the foursomes and ask each other questions, letting the autobiographies grow deeper.